CONTE

CHOICE

Richard Scott • *That Broke into Shining Crystals* • Faber

RECOMMENDATIONS

Dane Holt • *Father's Father's Father* • Carcanet Press
Charles Lang • *The Oasis* • Skein Press
Diane Seuss • *Modern Poetry* • Fitzcarraldo Editions
Desree • *Altar* • Bad Betty Press

SPECIAL COMMENDATION

Oluwaseun Olayiwola • *Strange Beach* • Fitzcarraldo Editions

TRANSLATION CHOICE

Anna Akhmatova • *In Love and Revolution: Selected Poems*
Translated by Stephen Capus
Shearsman Books

PAMPHLET CHOICE

Troy Cabida • *Symmetric of Bone: Poems after Elsa Peretti*
Fourteen Poems

Poetry Book Society

CHOICE SELECTORS RECOMMENDATION SPECIAL COMMENDATION	YOMI ṢODE & VICTORIA KENNEFICK
TRANSLATION SELECTOR	SHIVANEE RAMLOCHAN
PAMPHLET SELECTORS	YOUSIF M. QASMIYEH & ALYCIA PIRMOHAMED
CONTRIBUTORS	SOPHIE O'NEILL MEGAN ROBSON LEDBURY CRITICS
EDITORIAL & DESIGN	ALICE KATE MULLEN

Poetry Book Society Memberships
Choice
4 Books a Year: 4 Choice books & 4 *Bulletins* (UK £65, Europe £85, ROW £120)
World
8 Books: 4 Choices, 4 Translation books & 4 *Bulletins* (£98, £160, £190)
Complete
24 Books: 4 Choices, 16 Recommendations, 4 Translations & 4 *Bulletins* (£230, £290, £360)
Single copies of the *Bulletin* £12.99
Cover Artwork: *Rainbow Cannonball* by Marie Cameron
www.mariecameronstudio.com
Copyright Poetry Book Society and contributors. All rights reserved.
ISBN 9781913129750   ISSN 0551-1690

Poetry Book Society | Milburn House | Dean Street | Newcastle upon Tyne | NE1 1LF
0191 230 8100 | enquiries@poetrybooksociety.co.uk

WWW.POETRYBOOKS.CO.UK

LETTER FROM THE PBS

Congratulations to Richard Scott for receiving the Choice selection for his second collection, *That Broke into Shining Crystals*. I hope these Spring Recommendations will introduce some new poets and publishers to you. Beyond Richard Scott, we have four debut collections in our selections: Desree, Dane Holt and Charles Lang alongside Oluwaseun Olayiwola, our Special Commendation. If these poets are new to you, I hope you enjoy the samples of their work and are tempted to check out their collections!

Interestingly to me, many of the selected poets are alumni of fellowships, scholarships or initiatives to promote art. While we sit back and read the best poetry that UK and Irish publishers have to offer, it's worth considering how these amazing writers have honed their craft. There is a whole world out there of writer development and support, helping tomorrow's prize-winners and bestsellers on their journey to become critically acclaimed writers and artists. It's really wonderful to see our PBS recommended poets having come through these processes, which are extremely competitive to be accepted on to in the first place. (Full disclosure, when wearing another hat I am the Chair of a writer development organisation, the brilliant Writing Squad, so I have a strong interest in how writers become writers!). I would like to propose a toast to the unsung leaders of artist development programmes, from high profile scholarships to community writing groups, who help make the literature environment we inhabit so vibrant and diverse.

We'll be celebrating our PBS Spring Selections here in Newcastle on the 27th February with an event at Newcastle University featuring Oluwaseun Olayiwola and our new selector Yomi Ṣode – do come along if you can! And don't forget we have our quarterly podcast in partnership with Arji's Poetry Pickle Jar, an in-depth conversation with each season's Choice poet (scan the QR code below to listen).

We would really like to hear from you and have included a paper questionnaire in this *Bulletin* for those who are unable to access the internet. If you haven't completed the questionnaire online already, please do complete and return the paper copy to our address (listed adjacent). We would love to know more about you, our valued members, and what we can do to improve our offer to you.

SOPHIE O'NEILL
PBS & INPRESS DIRECTOR

THE 2025 SELECTORS

"I hope you journey with these books. Each of them unlocks new understanding to existing themes with care, humour and lived experience."

YOMI ṢODE
BOOK SELECTOR

Yomi Ṣode is a Nigerian British writer. His debut *Manorism* (Penguin, 2022) was adapted for stage at the Southbank Centre. He was shortlisted for the Rathbones Folio Prize 2023, the T.S. Eliot Prize 2022, the Brunel International African Poetry Prize 2021 and received the 2019 Jerwood Compton Poetry Fellowship. His acclaimed one-man show *COAT* toured nationally to sold-out audiences. In 2020 his libretto *Remnants*, performed with Chineke! Orchestra, premiered on BBC Radio 3. In 2021, his play, *and breathe…* premiered at the Almeida Theatre. Yomi is a Complete Works alumnus, a member of Malika's Poetry Kitchen and founder of BoxedIN, First Five, The Daddy Diaries and 12 in 12.

"What better way to celebrate seasonal rebirth and symbolic renewal than with the Spring 2025 Poetry Book Society Selections – in each of them I know you'll find a brilliant light to banish any of winter's lingering dark crevices."

VICTORIA KENNEFICK
BOOK SELECTOR

Victoria Kennefick grew up in Cork and lives in Kerry. Her debut *Eat or We Both Starve* (Carcanet Press, 2021) won the Seamus Heaney First Collection Poetry Prize and the Dalkey Book Festival Emerging Writer of the Year Award. It was shortlisted for the T.S. Eliot Prize, the Costa Poetry Book Award, Derek Walcott Prize for Poetry, and the Butler Literary Prize. She was the UCD/Arts Council of Ireland Writer-in-Residence 2023 and Poet-in-Residence at the Yeats Society Sligo 2022-24. Her poems appeared in *Poetry Magazine, PN Review, The Poetry Review, Poetry London, The Stinging Fly,* and more.

— SHIVANEE RAMLOCHAN —
— TRANSLATION SELECTOR —

Shivanee Ramlochan is a Trinidadian writer. Her debut *Everyone Knows I Am a Haunting* (Peepal Tree Press) was shortlisted for the Forward Prize. Her poems are anthologised in *100 Queer Poems* (Faber); *After Sylvia* (Nine Arches Press) and *Across Borders: New Poetry from the Commonwealth* (Verve Poetry Press).

— ARJI MANUELPILLAI —
— PODCAST HOST —

Arji Manuelpillai published his debut pamphlet *Mutton Rolls* with Out-Spoken Press. He is a member of Malika's Poetry Kitchen and was a Jerwood Arvon Mentee. Arji's debut *Improvised Explosive Device* was published by Penned in the Margins. He hosts the quarterly PBS podcast.

— YOUSIF M. QASMIYEH —
— PAMPHLET SELECTOR —

Born and educated in Baddawi refugee camp in Lebanon, Yousif M. Qasmiyeh is a poet and translator with a doctorate from the University of Oxford. His debut *Writing the Camp* (Broken Sleep Books) was a PBS Recommendation and shortlisted for the Ondaatje Prize, followed by *Eating the Archive* (Broken Sleep Books).

— ALYCIA PIRMOHAMED —
— PAMPHLET SELECTOR —

Alycia Pirmohamed is the author of the PBS Recommendation *Another Way to Split Water,* Pamphlet Choice *Hinge* and a Nan Shepherd prize winning non-fiction book *A Beautiful and Vital Place*. She teaches at the University of Cambridge and co-founded the Scottish BPOC Writers Network.

TEAM PBS

RICHARD SCOTT

Richard Scott was born in London in 1981. His first book *Soho* (Faber & Faber, 2018), was a Gay's the Word Book of the Year and was shortlisted for the T.S. Eliot Prize among other awards. He teaches poetry at the Faber Academy and is a lecturer in creative writing at Goldsmiths, University of London, where he also runs a poetry reading group. Richard is a fellow of the Royal Society of Literature, and his poetry has been translated into German and French.

THAT BROKE INTO SHINING CRYSTALS

FABER | £12.99 | PBS PRICE £9.75

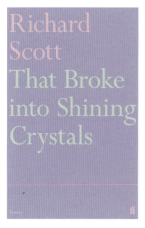

More times than often, I squint my eyes in envy whenever I see a good title, then hope with every fibre of my being that what I'm presented with (whether music, film or book) delivers. Richard Scott leaves little room to warm you into *That Broke into Shining Crystals,* the second poetry collection from a writer who weaves vulnerability with imagery, and explores personal accounts in fascinating yet intricate ways.

The sequencing in this collection, for example, is intentional, the poet carries on until there is nothing left and is that the ask? To give as much as you can in allowing us to feel what needs to be felt.

'Still Life with Bananas' opens with:

> curved like dicks they sit – cosy in wicker – an orgy
> of total yellowness – all plenty and arching – beyond

Then ends with:

> ...just
> once I want to see a banana that looks like a dick
> and laugh – just once I want to see a dick and not think about you.

A poem on heartbreak, with so much more happening in between. The final sequence juxtaposes the different forms of crystals, its beauty, so visceral you could imagine holding each one in the palm of your hand. The weight of these poems knocking against, consoling and, at times, shattering to let the light in.

What's striking in this collection is the poet's ability to play with structure. We are guided, following the rules created by Scott. Of course, when considering the heightened nature of some of the themes explored, you're left considering the fragility of self. The pristine and the broken, what is being masked, what people see, and a type of freeness excavated through past trauma. *That Broke into Shining Crystals* is as experimental as it is luminous. A welcomed return for fans and new readers.

YOMI ṢODE

RICHARD SCOTT

I think *That Broke into Shining Crystals* is, maybe, trying to investigate how to talk, write or sing about trauma and hurt when you don't have access to normative language with which to express yourself. The speaker in these poems cannot say, exactly, what has happened to them. There is no template to describe grooming and abuse. Also, they've been told not to say anything. And speaking directly might be too painful.

There are three interlocking sections in the book which look at this idea in slightly different lights. Firstly, through ekphrasis. Using the symbols of still life paintings – lemons, oysters, lobster, a single grape – the speaker experiences a kind of heightened lyric revelation that won't quit. Every painting is an unearthing. Maybe he feels similarly arranged, frozen in varnish. Here, I was really moved and inspired by the still lifes of Margareta Haverman, Rachel Ruysch and Jean Baptiste Siméon Chardin amongst others.

Then there's 'Coy' – a long found poem, a vocabularyclept – which repurposes the lexicon of Andrew Marvell's 'To His Coy Mistress'. Maybe I found some boldness in using someone else's language; it perhaps engendered speaking out further. But the speaker is also concerned with not speaking: "I long for sound – I long for not sound." Maybe it was also about listening, dictation, too – Marvell's music and carpe diem philosophy felt transformative.

Finally, there's the title sequence – twenty two crystals which all speak back to Arthur Rimbaud's *Illuminations* but through the prism of crystals, gemstones and geology, and their related scientific and New Age languages. I guess the crystal poems are a kind of intralingual or experiential translation. But they're also about looking for some wisdom and help from a queer ancestor who might be a kind of "shamanic" guide. Maybe there's also this attempt to try and envision a post-trauma, crystalline, landscape. The speaker says, "these wounds are new eyes", and maybe I've come to believe that.

RICHARD RECOMMENDS

Emily Berry, *Unexhausted Time* (Faber); Mei-mei Berssenbrugge, *A Treatise on Stars* (New Directions); Tom Betteridge, *Dog Shades* (Just Not); Wanda Coleman, *Bathwater Wine* (Black Sparrow Press); Peter Gizzi, *Archeophonics* (Wesleyan); Bonnie Hancell, *In This Allegory / Where We Disappear* (death of workers); Daljit Nagra, *Indiom* (Faber); Hoa Nguyen, *Red Juice* (Wave); Alice Notley, *Being Reflected Upon* (Penguin); Rebecca Perry, *On Trampolining* (Makina); Camille Ralphs, *After You Were, I am* (Faber); Denise Riley, *Dry Air* (Virago); Cecilia Vicuña, *Spit Temple* (Ugly Duckling).

EMERALD

for Emily Berry

    On the hillside little boys are twirling and looping and catching the light and falling down into the grass which is the colour of raw emeralds, shifting and bright.
    The field is a body. Wild grass rippling over breasts and muscles, the jut of a hipbone. Some of the grass is trampled down into mud like a battlefield – screams catch the air. Some of the grass is spread over little hillocks like shallow graves. Some of the grass is cut into a bit, desire lines and goat paths, leading to all the places you ever dreamed of going but didn't.
    Emerald grass at your feet and an emerald seam in the sky constellated by flickers, green pictures. The light is innocent, primitive. Its green ray aids – unearthing, X-raying.
    The little boys are tearing up fistfuls of emerald grass and throwing it into the air and dancing in the green and prismatic rain. The little boys themselves seem green and made of emerald – more fairy than boy. Crystalline, detoxifying – these ones are shining.
    All the greens are very close to your face right now. The landscape holds you like a basket. Overcome. There is no abyss just this immense patience. Recovery is possible.

STILL LIFE WITH PLUMS, MELON, PEACHES AND MOSS-COVERED BRANCHES

And all those plums, a startling shade of thunder – like
look at the bloom on those plums! I never understood before
how you could call discolouration, this full body scar,
a bloom, blossom. And a melon in shadow like something
that hasn't been grasped yet like how maybe transference
sends me into the arms of these difficult men who will hurt me
and not let me heal. Maybe. How to be happy when happy
is not even a thing. I want to be like these three peaches
you haven't even noticed yet. Each one a yolky ginger dawn
coming up and tinting everything this crackled gold. O
to be peachy keen! I will be again. And it's not my fault
that he found me because I was moss-green, downy, singing
of life – like these branches, the last symbol, that snap me open
with a kind of just-been-carried-in-from-the-garden realism.
Still life yet still growing. So keep on growing, Richard.

Image: George Lawrence

DESREE

Desree is an award-winning writer, spoken word artist, educator and producer based in London and Slough. An alumna of BORN::FREE Writers Collective, Jerwood Arts and the Obsidian Foundation, Desree was Poet in Residence at Glastonbury Festival 2022 and Slough's EMPOWORD. A familiar voice on BBC Radio Berkshire, her work has been broadcast on Radio 4's *The Life and Rhymes of Benjamin Zephaniah*; and published in *JOY// US Poems of Queer Joy*, *Ink Sweat & Tears*, Spoken Word London's *Anti-Hate Anthology* and more. She performs across the UK and internationally. Her pamphlet *I Find My Strength in Simple Things* was published by Burning Eye Books in 2021.

I RECOMMENDATION

ALTAR

BAD BETTY PRESS | £10.99 | PBS PRICE £8.25

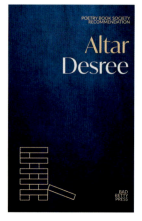

Altar, the debut collection from the poet Desree, is gorgeous in its redefining of self. I enjoyed the placements the poet positions us in. We are either lamenting in Slough, feeling the impact of Black British identity, or reeling off a Dizzee Rascal lyric, a nod to the communities who pick up the nuances tucked in the nook of these poems.

An important thing to highlight is the resilience sifting through the collection. Though there might be similar checkpoints in our lives, no story is the same. I don't read poetry collections hoping for a happy ever after, I want an understanding of the "how", in order for me to know my next steps in this thing called life.

In 'tell yourself', Desree navigates the complex nature of love between family, friends, and partner. The observation and uncomfortable conversations that have yet to happen. An inner joy waiting to burst at the seams into a reality that may not be as welcoming.

While in 'Stop That', we are met with various personal accounts within the framework of an iconic Grime reference (if you know, you know) interspersed in between.

> Got drunk on the Cutty Sark.
> Bought a house. Made gun
> fingers out of bruised hands

Altar, in its subtlety, opens the world to heartbreak, spirituality, choice and consent. The poet is faced with situations where it could go in one of many ways. Not many are as ready to make a sacrifice, not many are as ready to face what their backs have been turned to for so long. Desree is not asking the reader to jump straight into any type of action after reading. This is a collection to take some time over; a collection that probes how to claim back what is rightfully yours.

SELECTOR'S COMMENT

YOMI ṢODE

DESREE

Altar is my debut poetry collection, and at its heart, it is an exploration of sacrifice, particularly within Black womanhood. I wanted to dive into the sacrifices society demands – from emotional labour to navigating systemic barriers – and those we make to ensure we survive. These poems became snapshots of what it means to journey towards something resembling freedom, pausing to reflect on both the struggles and the beauty in it all.

It is an ode to the unyielding power of Black womanhood, the messiness of family – both chosen and inherited – and the ways gentrification reshapes our sense of place. The poems simultaneously hold moments of joy, tension, and tenderness as they grapple with faith, queerness and contradiction.

For me, this collection is about reclamation: of self, of space, of stories. I invite readers to come with me, to confront the storms and celebrate the small but mighty victories. I have tried to write this collection and these poems so many times. At times I thought I had laid bare my own weaknesses, fears, and aspirations, and I had created something truly vulnerable (believe me, I had not). Despite my efforts, I realised that what I thought was vulnerability fell short. It became apparent that I had been attempting to manufacture vulnerability in a way that allowed me to feel comfortable, rather than delving deeper.

Through this collection, I've come to understand that true vulnerability requires a willingness to confront discomfort and uncertainty, to take risks and start again as many times as necessary. As I continue to push the boundaries of my work, I do so with renewed courage and conviction, fuelled by the understanding that true vulnerability is the catalyst for genuine connection and is, in itself, a form of protest.

DESREE RECOMMENDS

Rachel Long, *My Darling From The Lions* (Picador); Gboyega Odubanjo, *Adam* (Faber); Kareem Parkins-Brown, *Oi You Lot* (Little Betty); Caleb Femi, *The Wickedest* (4th Estate); Antonia Jade King, *She Too Is a Sailor* (Little Betty); Courtney Conrad, *I Am Evidence* (Bloodaxe Books); Yomi Ṣode, *Manorism* (Penguin); Raymond Antrobus, *The Perseverance* (Penned in the Margins); Yrsa Daley-Ward, *Bone* (Penguin); Malika Booker, *Breadfruit* (flipped eye publishing); Roger Robinson, *A Portable Paradise* (Peepal Tree Press); Lalah-Simone Springer, *An Aviary of Common Birds* (Broken Sleep Books).

Today,

i do not want to jump off anything
a building is just a building

INTRUDERS

  1992, I arrived with a body too small to carry anything but concrete and chimneys. I returned each year and just like they had taught me in school, called it *mine*.

Anguilla was first home to Indigenous Amerindian peoples who put home on their back and roved from South America.

  I buried my tongue under the accent hoping to abstract the coral and limestone. I built sandcastles by oceans clear enough to see the red, white and blue anchors. Telling stories of a motherland to the children she had tried to drown.

Some claim Columbus was the first marauder of these sands, whiter than the hands of its thieves.

  Oh, small island people. Do you not hear the settler in this accent? How I have come here to take what does not belong to me, name it ancestry. All I know of this land is what my grandmother taught me, we courtesy to the same Queen.

Others claim it was René Goulaine de Laudonnière

  Oh, small island people, with hair as straight as rulers, they consumed everything, took what wasn't offered, planted tobacco and sugar in your bloodline and claimed ignorance when the cancer spread.

Malliouhana, Arrow-head, they took your name, then baptised you eel, slippery, mysterious, needing to be caught.

DANE HOLT

Dane Holt holds a PhD from Queen's University Belfast. His debut pamphlet *Many Professional Wrestlers Never Retire* (Lifeboat Press) was published in 2023 and was a Poetry Book Society Autumn Pamphlet Choice. In 2019, he won the inaugural Brotherton Prize, awarded by the University of Leeds. He was the 2023 Ciaran Carson Publishing Fellow at the Seamus Heaney Centre, Belfast.

FATHER'S FATHER'S FATHER

CARCANET | £11.99 | PBS PRICE £9.00

Dane Holt's remarkable debut with Carcanet Press opens with an unexpected and completely surprising cameo from American Professional wrestler, bodybuilder, actor and rapper, John Cena. Full of contradictions, the poem navigates themes of masculinity, violence, perfectionism, repression and celebrity. The first line echoes many of the collections concerns, 'Everything you do you do precisely.' In the poem, Cena's celebrity is interrogated as edgeless and obvious, but innately menacing, his blankness reflecting all that is problematic about the patriarchal, colonial, capitalist project:

> Often, when it comes to your
> distinctive brand of violence, John,
> less is more
> and none is more than enough.

It is a bold and inspired choice that sets the tone for the remainder of the collection that is by turns tragic and comedic, challenging readers to enter these conflicting states with ease facilitated by Holt's considerable skill and lyrical dexterity throughout:

> We all have problems. Yours
> the decline of luxury air travel.
> Mine the dog that followed me
> home from the funeral.

Death, loss and grief – personal, social and ecological in nature – are central to the collection's focus, yet Holt brings a lightness of touch to even the darkest of moments. The effect is witty, inventive, compelling and original, embodied by speakers and characters who are both breathtakingly articulate yet often frustratingly unaware of the true nature of their vulnerabilities. This makes for a moving and illuminating read that is convincing in tone with disciplined and precise lines, that are surreal, rebellious and chaotic, in turn. It is a brilliant and bold debut that interrogates the fragile nature of masculinity, generational trauma and the relationship between the individual, family and community in revelatory ways:

> I could
> do anything. I could do anything. I could do anything.
> What do you make of that? The answer can be nothing.

SELECTOR'S COMMENT | VICTORIA KENNEFICK

DANE HOLT

It's difficult to know what people will find interesting in your work. One of the things I find interesting is that my book begins with the word "Everything" and ends with the word "Nothing". (Would you believe me if I said this was intentional?) I like poems that try to contain everything the poet can lay their hands on, and poems that conjure themselves out of nothing. Hopefully this book lends something to each category.

Many of these poems are narratives and most take place in the aftermath of some unspecified calamitous event. Social, personal, ecological. I hope you won't take this as slackness on my part, a half-finished job. I don't subscribe to many definites when it comes to writing poems, but one of the things I know is that my poetry needs to happen in the aftermath or the meanwhile. The poem must remove itself, take stock, redoubt, and then rejoin history.

I was once asked to come up with a definition of the difference between poetry and prose. Immediately I thought, poetry is pool, prose is snooker, but I couldn't justify it. The best I could do was a scene from *It's a Wonderful Life*, the scene where the guardian angel reveals himself to George Bailey as they're drying off in the toll collector's cabin. George doesn't believe the angel at first and has to be convinced of his own reality. I think that's prose. But there's someone else who saw the angel. The toll collector. He falls off his chair when he learns the truth and disappears into the night. Where does he go? Who does he see and how does he tell them what he's seen? Why won't anyone believe him? The toll collector is poetry.

DANE RECOMMENDS

Anthony (Vahni) Capildeo, *Skin Can Hold* (Carcanet); Leontia Flynn, *Taking Liberties* (Cape); James Tate, *The Eternal Ones of the Dream: Selected Poems 1990-2010* (Ecco); Jane Yeh, *The Ninjas* (Carcanet); Terrance Hayes, *How to be Drawn* (Penguin); Matthew Sweeney, *The Bridal Suite* (Cape); Cathy Park Hong, *Engine Empire* (Norton); Geoff Hattersley, *Harmonica* (Wrecking Ball); Diane Seuss, *Modern Poetry* (Fitzcarraldo); Jericho Brown, *The Tradition* (Picador); Tony Harrison, *Collected Poems* (Penguin); Dorothy Malloy, *Hare Soup* (Faber); Ciaran Carson, *Still Life* (Gallery); Larry Levis, *Elegy* (Pittsburgh).

a fresh pitch, shed
your previous skin.
If in doubt,

'THE GRANARIES ARE BURSTING WITH MEAL'

Your father's father's father
poisoned a beautiful horse,
that's the story. Now you know this
you've opened the door marked
'Family History'. Behind it

a man is scratching a name
you don't recognise into the ice
which surrounds him; his six sons burn
the memory of six brothers
as midnight oil. Unhurried

as the death of a poisoned horse,
and without gesture to each other,
they begin to move. They don't
have far to go, they travel light,
having no horse.

As they get closer to you, their backs
straighten, their clothes begin to mend.
Their faces soften the way
faces that have never seen
a city at night soften. Soon the father

looks the same age as the sons.
But the sons are lost in the city.
Now this is the story. A father
is looking furiously in the city
for six sons that don't want to be found.

CHARLES LANG

Charles Lang is from Glasgow. His poems have appeared in numerous publications including *Poetry Ireland Review, Poetry London, The Poetry Review* and *The Stinging Fly*. He was selected for the Poetry Ireland Introductions series in 2022. In 2024, he was Ciaran Carson Writing and the City Fellow at the Seamus Heaney Centre, Queen's University Belfast, and was shortlisted for the Edwin Morgan Poetry Award.

THE OASIS

SKEIN PRESS | £10.00 | PBS PRICE £7.50

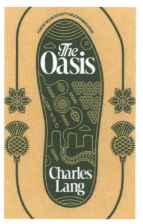

That's the thing with story, you tap into a rich enough voice and soon you'll find yourself immersed within it, complicit almost as though you are right next to the speaker. As outlandish as that sounds, that's the feeling Charles Lang pulls out of the reader in *The Oasis*, his debut poetry collection published by Skein Press. There's confidence in being able to world-build. No, this is no *Stranger Things*, but it's easy to visualise the goings-on with our lead narrator, as each story starts.

Not everybody's experience is your experience, and not every poem has to have layers of complexity for a set of poetry elites to understand. However, what Lang does so brilliantly is to recreate the experiences and complexities of a community of people who understand the undercurrent of chaos, the working-class lives of his family, friends, and survival.

'The Chase', the first poem in the collection opens like a movie:

> Aw it takes is a wee 'fuck the polis' n a night ae excitement is on:
> the chase, navigatin side streets n gable ends, hidin in bushes,

While 'Nightclub' reminds me of my nights out with all the mandem, using colloquialisms I lean into in my own work.

> It builds sloooowly then fuck ye! it explodes fae naewhere.
> A wee surprise. The dancefler erupts. The DJ knows
> wit she's daein. She's playin the crowd like a fiddle, as if
> controllin the fate ae the night is an average kickaboot.
> She's cool as fuck.

I enjoyed being an outsider looking in, championing the culture explored in *The Oasis*, its uncompromising and authentic nature, whether lived or not, surging through each poem. Memories and moments. This book makes me want to search for my notebook, head down to my local park, sit down and map out the happenings within the time I'm there. It brings me back to grassroots and connecting with what intrinsically is me.

SELECTOR'S COMMENT

YOMI ṢODE

CHARLES LANG

The collection, straightforwardly, is a sequence of minor events that have taken place during my life; real or imagined. I wanted in some way to reflect the marginalisation of working-class people and communities, but in writing I was aware of the limitations my own experience brings and therefore the poems that make up the collection are only truly representative of myself, or whatever it is that was in my head.

Having lived as a working-class person for my entire existence, and having been recently in the worlds of higher education and literary culture, explorations of social class and its bearing on education or art or poetry were inevitable and became central to what I was writing. The language of the poems is imitative of how I think and understand the world, somewhere between vernacular English and demotic Scots, as variable and inconsistent as that can be. I don't intend for it to be anything other than how I speak.

I hope that the poems offer more than their explorations of class, however, and that they reflect more broadly what it is like to live at the present moment. I wanted to explore the city. Much of the collection was written whilst I was living in Ireland, and so the negotiation of home is something that changes throughout, particularly since the latter part was written whilst I was (re)establishing a new life in Scotland with my wife. It is maybe about family as much as it is about anything else. The climate crisis was at the forefront of my mind when I wrote these poems and in many ways that's what I think most of them might be about. Likewise our relationships with animals. Or football. Coffee. Walking in the park.

CHARLES RECOMMENDS

Colin Bramwell, *Fower Pessoas* (Carcanet); Nidhi Zak/Aria Eipe, *Auguries of a Minor God* (Faber); Patrick James Errington, *The Swailing* (McGill-Queens); Jake Hawkey, *But & Though* (Picador); Patrick Romero McCafferty, *glass knot sun* (ignition); Mícheál McCann, *Devotion* (Gallery); Scott McKendry, *Gub* (Corsair); Majed Mujed, trans. Kareem James Abu-Zeid, *The Book of Trivialities* (Skein); David Nash, *No Man's Land* (Dedalus); Yousif M. Qasmiyeh, *Writing the Camp* (Broken Sleep); Shane Strachan, *DWAMS* (Tapsalteerie); Kandace Siobhan Walker, *Cowboy* (Cheerio); Roseanne Watt, *Moder Dy* (Polygon).

Image: Patrick Fisher, Frontwards Design

GLASGOW SONNETS

iii.

I know the city by its limits,
O Glaschu!
I see it in ma dreams
at dusk:
the view fae the Cathkin Braes.
Light up Ardencraig,
light up Ballantay,
Machrie,
Queen's Park,
the Kelvin.
Dear green place,
I come n go n go
tae come back. I come back
fur yer every possibility

Image: Gabrielle Montesanti

DIANE SEUSS

Diane Seuss is the author of six books of poetry, including *Modern Poetry*; *frank: sonnets*, winner of the Pulitzer Prize, the National Book Critics Circle Award, the Los Angeles Times Book Prize, and the PEN/Voelcker Prize; *Still Life With Two Dead Peacocks and a Girl*, a finalist for the National Book Critics Circle Award and the Los Angeles Times Book Prize; and *Four-Legged Girl*, a finalist for the Pulitzer Prize. She was a 2020 Guggenheim Fellow, and in 2021 she received the John Updike Award from the American Academy of Arts and Letters. She lives in Michigan.

MODERN POETRY

FITZCARRALDO EDITIONS | £12.99 | PBS PRICE £9.75

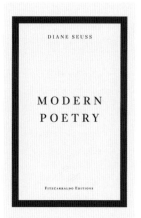

The politics of compilation regarding literary anthologies is necessarily fraught with contemporary concerns about inclusivity, balance and fairness which bring new perspectives and a more equitable lens through which to critique established and canonical texts. American poet, Diane Seuss' latest collection *Modern Poetry*, her sixth book, takes its title from one such volume, in this case the first textbook Seuss encountered as a child as well as the name of the first poetry course she took in college.

It is an inspired conceit because it allows Seuss to not only explore her initial anxiety regarding her relationship with poetry, but also allows her to serve up a multiplicity of forms representing the broad landscape suggested by the book's title, including the ballad, fugue, coda, refrain and aria. The result is a thrilling exploration of metapoetics – a symphony of language where the poems, deeply aware of themselves, facilitate Seuss' ferocious interrogation of her own proximity to art but also move through form, beyond inherent human defensiveness, to embody a new more open-hearted definition of love.

The collection opens with epigraphs by John Keats, Wallace Stevens, and Gwendolyn Brooks and their inclusion forefronts Seuss' attention to legacy in American poetics. *Modern Poetry* begins with 'Little Fugue State' where the speaker describes poetry as "this dog I've walked and walked / to death" and forefronts Seuss' concerns regarding the project of poetry. In classical music "fugue" means "escape" or "flight" and there is a sense that pervades the book that poetry can be used as a means of escape but also it is very much a flight into the true nature of what is. In one of the book's final poems 'Love Letter' the speaker proclaims,

> I have worked it all out in front of you.
> (...)
> This is a love letter.

Modern Poetry is a fascinating personal anthology of the poets and poems that have shaped Seuss' moving and arresting thematic vision and in it she firmly positions herself as one of the most original of the modern poets writing today.

SELECTOR'S COMMENT

VICTORIA KENNEFICK

DIANE SEUSS

Modern Poetry begins with 'Little Fugue State', referencing the musical fugue and the psychological fugue, characterized by dissociation, amnesia, and wandering. My disorientation arose from the pandemic years, which transformed what I used to call solitude into isolation. Rising tyranny begat in me a gnawing question: What can poetry mean now? To question my sole companion, more steadfast than any friend, lover, or even dog, ushered me to a painful edge, and the only means I had to talk myself back from it was the subject itself – poetry. The poems wander back to my cobbled education in the rural, working-class place where I was raised, imagining their way into romanticism and modernism, arguing for the uselessness of art, and ultimately reconceptualizing my relationship with poetry and with love.

When I consider the inception of *Modern Poetry*, what I see is the spine of a small book, one of several texts on the bookshelves my mother built after my father died from a rare illness, the result of his exposure to asbestos during World War II. She had not been allowed to go to college, and did not have a way to make a living, with two kids to support on a small stipend from Social Security. Thus, she decided to go get educated. I was an early reader. I'd sit on the floor in front of her schoolbooks, the spines lined up like keys on a toy piano, each with its color and tone: Joyce. Conrad. Byron. Shelley. Keats. No one non-white, and only one female, Virginia Woolf. How might my mother's education have resonated for her if it had been otherwise? Still, there it was, the small book with a fragile spine, cherry red and blossom white, beyond my grasp, but willing to wait for me: *Modern Poetry*.

DIANE RECOMMENDS

Kenzie Allen, *Cloud Missives* (Tin House Books); Oliver de la Paz, *The Diaspora Sonnets* (Liveright); Cass Donish, *Your Dazzling Death* (Knopf); Jane Huffman, *Public Abstract* (American Poetry Review); Jennifer Franklin, *If Some God Shakes Your House* (Four Way Books); Joan Kwon Glass, *Daughter of Three Gone Kingdoms* (Perugia Press); Oksana Maksymchuk, *Still City: Diary of an Invasion* (Carcanet Press); Maggie Millner, *Couplets: A Love Story* (Farrar, Straus and Giroux); Evie Shockley, *the new black* (Wesleyan Poetry Series).

LITTLE FUGUE STATE

Far have I wandered not knowing
the names of where,
long have I woven this dress
of human hair, here
I have pitched my tent, here and there,
not knowing my name,
or where, not even the color of my hair
nor why
it tangles so, nor where my comb goes,
nor where my brush,
how far I wandered through underbrush,
into onrush,
nor where my body was, nor what it called
itself, nor the nature
of my calling, nor what my scrawling meant,
not that scrawl then,
nor this scrawl here, nor what a self
could be,
nor what a bee could be, nor breath,
nor poetry,
this dog I've walked and walked
to death.

CODA

The best poem is no poem.
In a swath of poems, or a swathe of poems,
the best poem is without genealogy or fragrance.

It's like an animal born without a voice box.
Or its inconvenient voice box has been removed.

The best body, nobody says to no one, is no body.
The best body, no body at all.
The sound a bodiless body makes

is akin to the sound a bird makes when it dips
its beak into a cup of jam.

Sometimes a bone makes a sound when it breaks.
It sounds just as you'd imagine it would sound.
Other times the bone is as quiet

as a really good burglar breaking and entering.
There used to be a prairie that extended way past

the ending of every story. An expanse of sedges and grasses
and wind, which made a sound like a sprinkler when the water
has been turned off for the nonpayment of the bill.

The what? The bill. The unpaid water bill. Out of the spigot
streams a thirsty noncompliance. An antisong.

Image: Jury Dominguez

OLUWASEUN OLAYIWOLA

Oluwaseun (Seun) Olayiwola is a poet, critic, performer and choreographer based in London. His creative and critical work has been published in the *Guardian, The Poetry Review, PN Review, Oxford Poetry,* the *Telegraph*, the *TLS* and elsewhere. His choreographic work has been presented at the V&A, The Place, The Central School of Ballet, and Studio Voltaire. He has been commissioned by the Royal Society of Literature, Ledbury Poetry Festival, Southwark Council, and Studio 3 Arts. Seun has an MFA in Choreography from the Trinity Laban Conservatoire of Music and Dance, where he was a Fulbright Scholar in 2018-19. He recently began lecturing in dance in the Kingston School of Art. Seun is a member of the inaugural Rose Choreographic School at Sadler's Wells.

STRANGE BEACH

FITZCARRALDO EDITIONS | £ 12.99 | PBS PRICE £9.75

In the poem 'Strange Beach' which also gives its title to Oluwaseun Olayiwola's brilliant, stirring debut collection, the very first title in Fitzcarraldo's new poetry series, the poet states, "It's an opinion / the stars are unspoilable…" The poem unspools and unravels, whisking us from the celestial sphere to the seashore via everything in-between, so "sand is not sand but law." What is "unspoilable" is also, conversely, part of the human realm and therefore leads to an interrogation of performative and authentic methods of communicating with the self and with others.

Olayiwola's training as a choreographer informs the way the poems, which precede and follow on from this pivotal piece, ebb and flow as the interactions between the poems' speakers, predominantly two men, travel through themes of queer Black masculinity, death, parental relationships, coming-of-age experiences and love. The location of the poems changes too as the speakers explore and interrogate their various and shifting identities across oceans, geographies and within the complex netting of relationships on a macro and micro sphere. The waves of language and imagery shift and move into ever-more engrossing and engaging shapes that traverse the interior and exterior aspects of human experience through philosophical, abstract, intellectual and emotional explorations. The poem 'Strange Beach' ends with the line:

> No one can follow you here
> not having to become something else.

This is an essential trope of the collection, so expertly achieved in the dance between intellect and emotion, land and sea, earth and sky, exterior and interior, reality and appearances. While we are encouraged to enter a watery realm of uncertainty, while simultaneously feeling the sand between our toes, we are never abandoned by Olayiwola who urges us to move beyond survival and consider the reintegration of the more troubling parts of ourselves. It is a challenging move towards wholeness, as in the last lines of the poem 'Now' which close the collection:

> He slides his hand into my city
> and in my city
> his hand
> is disappeared.

VICTORIA KENNEFICK

POEM

You weren't invited to winter.

You showed up anyway,
asphalt weights around your wrists.

You took risks, you defined mercy
as survival, keeping the tested traditions
of your mother alive.

In reality she is not dead
but writing is, at best, protest.
Not protection.

You want to see to the end of the world,
you want a heartbeat of smoke
to pursue you like a voice
charmed out
by the universe's brass instrument,

want to think being swelled by tenor, by the soft lacquer
of beginnings, is to be safe from rust,
from necessary, because promised, wear.

Things for which there is
no technique
of preservation long enough—

It is not just your soul floundering
for permanence. The leaves are old crowns
rejecting the cobblestone
they are framed inside.

What will you do when they clear out?
What will you do when they are all but cleared out?

ANNA AKHMATOVA

STEPHEN CAPUS

Anna Akhmatova was born near Odesa, Ukraine, in 1889. In 1910 she married fellow poet Nikolay Gumilev and became associated with the literary movement known as Acmeism. The couple were divorced in 1918, three years before Gumilev was executed by the Bolsheviks for counter-revolutionary activities. Akhmatova achieved fame with her first collection of poems *Evening* in 1912, and consolidated her reputation as one of Russia's leading poets during the period preceding the October Revolution. Between the publication of the second edition of *Anno Domini* in 1923 and the death of Stalin in 1953 – with a brief reprieve during World War II – she found herself subject to censorship, and in 1946 she was expelled from the Soviet Writers' Union. Although she faced much personal hardship, she was also able to create *Requiem*, her great affirmation of solidarity with the victims of the Stalinist purges. After Stalin's death in 1953 the restrictions on Akhmatova's work were gradually relaxed and she published *The Course of Time* in 1958. She died in Moscow in 1966.

Stephen Capus studied Russian at Birmingham University and The School of Slavonic and East European Studies, London University. His translations have appeared in the *Penguin Book of Russian Poetry* (Penguin, 2015) and *Centres of Cataclysm* (Bloodaxe, 2016). His pamphlet *24 Hours* was published by Rack Press in 2020.

IN LOVE AND REVOLUTION
ANNA AKHMATOVA, TRANS. STEPHEN CAPUS
SHEARSMAN BOOKS | £12.95 | PBS PRICE £9.72

Within the formal paces of these poems beats an intemperate, ungovernable heart. *In Love and Revolution: Selected Poems* by Anna Akhmatova, translated from the Russian by Stephen Capus, gathers writing from across the decades of the celebrated poet's life, presenting them as essential windows into the work of a remarkable sociopolitical agitator – a fighter for desire and freedom alike.

Akhmatova's is a precise and unerring world. The images within it are crisp in their delineation, the mechanisms of the poems carrying them taut and composed. Form, the rigour and reliability of it, is the anchor to these verses, which hold in their grasp even the most inarticulable of human conditions. Consider the untitled poem from *Reed* (1924-1940), beginning "When someone dies all his portraits" which pinpoints with a dread accuracy the transformation – sepulchral, spectral, and something else entirely – that occurs when a beloved figure ceases to be. Even when least mappable, the dimensions of Akhmatova's poems are cut with a generous exactingness, an endless cavern of possibilities contained within its structural demarcations.

Capus' translations are determined to abide with the consistency and lyrical quality of Akhmatova as she was, so that, even though the poems feel like they are coming to us from another country, that is their strength, not their detraction. These rooms of oppression and solitude, of appetite and discipline, that the speakers of the poems walk through – that Akhmatova herself inhabited – become ours to know, in *Love and Revolution's* curation from seven volumes of the poet's body of work.

In her well-known 'Requiem' (1935-1940), the refrain of a dogged survival pulses like a renegade vein:

> We were thrown together in hell—and yet still I miss them,
> those random friends; and I wonder where they are

Even in death, Akhmatova's ghosts roam their territories with an unkillable immediacy.

SHIVANEE RAMLOCHAN

REQUIEM (AN EXTRACT)

And I'll never forget you, wherever I go,
Whatever new horrors I'm destined to know.

And even if one day they somehow suppress
My voice through which millions of lives were expressed,

I ask that you all still remember to pray
For my soul on the eve of my burial day.

And if in the future they give the command
To raise up a statue to me in this land,

I consent to this honour – but only so long
As they solemnly pledge not to place it upon

The shore of the sea by which I was born,
For my link with the sea has long since been torn;

Nor in the park of the Tsars, by the tree
Where a restless soul is still searching for me;

But to raise it instead near the prison's locked door
Where I waited for three hundred hours and more.

For I fear I'll forget in the vacuous peace
Of the grave that old woman who howled like a beast,

Or the rumbling wheels of the black prison vans,
Or the sound of the hateful jail door when it slammed.

And from motionless eyelids the melting snow,
Like tears, down my cheeks of bronze will flow

As the dove in the watchtower calls from on high
And the boats on the Neva go drifting on by.

TROY CABIDA

Troy Cabida is the author of *War Dove* (Bad Betty Press, 2020). His writing appears in *State of Play, Bi+ Lines, 100 Queer Poems*, and *Tiffany & Co.*, as well as being shortlisted for the Bridport Prize for Poetry 2024. He works for the National Poetry Library and holds a BA in Psychosocial Studies from Birkbeck, University of London. His debut collection is forthcoming with Nine Arches Press in 2025.

SYMMETRIC OF BONE
FOURTEEN   POEMS | £8.00 |

In Troy Cabida's *Symmetric of Bone: Poems after Elsa Peretti*, the body is an infinite text; it is written and rewritten, moulded and remoulded, queried and queered so the text should exist as both a singularity and plurality at the same time. This plurality is exactly where *Poems after Elsa Peretti* come to the fore, embodying a symmetry with the poet's own life as an organic extension of the other in their creative and ever-evolving self. In this way, what Italian designer Elsa Peretti did with jewellery becomes the correlative of what Cabida has so skilfully and texturally done in poetry: "to produce meaning / elsewhere".

The meaning that Cabida is seeking, is that of his queer body as it exists alongside other bodies but also as difference in its own right. As such, in this splendidly raw pamphlet, his body experiences the world corporeally by being part of it and in so doing it becomes an integral part of its deconstruction and reassembling:

> take the colour
> of rot   turn it
> into skin
> soft with desire

This lyrical engagement with the material object transforms these poems into sensorial voyages, saturated with varying materialities, textures and spaces, where senses seem to move from one sight/site to another without losing touch with their origins. Instead of being predicated on generics, Cabida's poetry leans on the corporeal and generational specificities by involving people (in particular the father), spaces and times in this expansive collage of experience and exposure. As I return to Cabida's *Symmetric of Bone* once again to regather my thoughts, I realise that it is Cabida's body and others' that I am reading and writing about. Poignant and above all "closer to skin than testament", these bodies write their own stories out of bodily fluids and memories, in order to grow and live for themselves.

> I will tend to the gap inside me
> the same way people do their gardens,
> children, other beloved objects.
> I will honour its flesh, its temporal,
> its animate that says my joy is in the knowing

SELECTOR'S COMMENT

YOUSIF M. QASMIYEH & ALYCIA PIRMOHAMED

PITCHER

After Hiro for Tiffany & Co., 1996

Laws of surrealism dictate
water be given abandon,
spill upwards
from a warm body
of metal, sheen so fresh
it's an open wound,
susceptible
to the slightest touch.

The reaching to the air
and the impossible
offers a multitude of interpretations:
water as elephant's ear,
dove's wing, part of an aeroplane
as imagined by a child
whose bubbling memory
is yet to be untangled from nature.

All of this stands on a thin river
made to be forgotten, to be laid upon
safely as in stagnant,
a kind of shelter
I'm learning to jump out of.

SPRING BOOK REVIEWS

DON MEE CHOI: HARDLY WAR
REVIEWED BY SHASH TREVETT

Using her father's work as a photojournalist in the Korean and Vietnam wars, Don Mee Choi's celebrated second collection is a mixture of poetry, memoir, puzzle and libretto. Hypnotic repetitions ("hardly" and "war" are dissected and re-negotiated throughout the book) and syncopated rhythms like a jazz score, dig with a primal insistence into meaning, as sound and cadences combine to make the mind zing. A complex and invigorating read, this collection extends the boundaries of both poetry and language.

AND OTHER STORIES | £14.99 | PBS PRICE £11.25

EMILY COTTERILL: SIGNIFICANT WOW
REVIEWED BY DAVE COATES

A paean to the boredom, alienation and petty fiefdoms of small-town adolescence in Alfreton, Derbyshire, Cotterill's best poems are, like Frost's New England pieces, deceptively plainspoken, with a deep note of loneliness sounding barely below the surface. In 'East Midlands Designer Outlet', the metaphor turns concrete, the eponymous mall literally built over a deep and disused mine. In its finest moments, *Significant Wow* feels more like a keen-eyed short story collection: deeply, movingly invested in the humanity of its subjects.

SEREN BOOKS | £ 10.99 | PBS PRICE £8.25

KAREN DOWNS-BARTON: MINX
REVIEWED BY SHASH TREVETT

A heart-breaking collection which explores the "inherited rootlessness" of a mixed Anglo-Romani-Caribbean heritage by way of bigotry, abuse, neglect and the British care system. There are no hiding places in the elasticity of this poet's mind. Skilfully weaving the Romani language through the memory of a fractured childhood, Downs-Barton manipulates words to contain the uncontainable, creating poems of such intense beauty and poignancy, such as 'Dear Faye'. This is a collection which deserves the best of our attention and respect.

CHATTO & WINDUS | £12.99 | PBS PRICE £9.75

LEDBURY CRITICS

PAUL FARLEY: WHEN IT RAINED FOR A MILLION YEARS
REVIEWED BY DAVE COATES

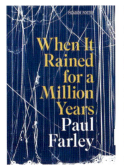

Veteran lyricist Farley returns with his signature blend of magical realism and nostalgia, a miscellany of observations on nature, meta-commentary on writing and publishing poetry, and artful reconstructions of his own past. There are tantalising brushes with social commentary: 'Three Riots' identifies Britain's history of police violence; it would've been fascinating to read more. Farley's strength, throughout his career, is in the delicacy of his poems' music, their soft lighting and good humour, and this book is no exception.

PICADOR | £12.99 | PBS PRICE £9.75

S.J. FOWLER: GOBLINS
REVIEWED BY DAVE COATES

Fowler's new book ends with 'Postscript', a tongue-in-cheek prose piece that pre-emptively defends *Goblins* against criticism before attacking the poetry/academia pipeline and its perceived censoriousness. It's an oddly sour end to a book that is mainly energetic, witty and conceptually creative. It makes the book's themes of mass surveillance and technological overreach feel retroactively small, messily conflating readers' critique and governmental censorship. Still, *Goblins* remains a fun read, with plenty of linguistic and comic flourish.

BROKEN SLEEP BOOKS | £9.99 | PBS PRICE £7.50

DANIEL HINDS: NEW FAMOUS PHRASES
REVIEWED BY DAVE COATES

Hinds' playful and irreverent debut mines the great names of the English canon for its subjects, tone, and wordplay, in particular Ted Hughes. The book's imagination is impressively, almost claustrophobically weighty – it dreams of multiple apocalypses – though its themes often feel insubstantial, as if the words themselves mattered more than what they signify. Two prose-poem responses to Jay Bernard and Terrance Hayes are somewhat misjudged, but Hinds' dedication to language-play is admirable, even when overshadowed by his heroes.

BROKEN SLEEP BOOKS | £12.99 | PBS PRICE £9.75

SABA KERAMATI: SELF-MYTHOLOGY
REVIEWED BY DAVE COATES

Keramati's first collection is elegant, thoughtful and precise, a lyrical exploration of her cultural inheritances (her mother is Chinese, her father Iranian, both are refugees). Among its highlights are the jagged, nightmarish 'The God Who Ate His Children', or the palpable heartache of 'Rewrite: I Go Back', in which the poet imagines preventing her parents from meeting. A few poems feel safe, a little too cautious with their images or premises, but *Self-Mythology* remains a rich, engaging and promising debut.

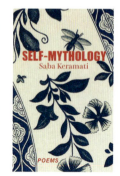

THE 87 PRESS | £12.99 | PBS PRICE £9.75

NICK MAKOHA: THE NEW CARTHAGINIANS
REVIEWED BY DAVE COATES

It's easy to focus on Makoha's formal ingenuity – adapting Jean-Michel Basquiat's "exploded collage" technique to poetry – far harder to map the astonishing horizons these tools enable. *The New Carthaginians* feels like an attempt to wrestle with the meaning of an imperial world which devastated the poet's native Uganda, and now offers (conditional) refuge; what can art do with such inescapable double-binds? The book's preoccupations with flight, Icarus, and stargazing are only the surface artefacts of a visceral, unrelenting, internal odyssey.

PENGUIN PRESS | £12.99 | PBS PRICE £9.75

FERNANDO PESSOA: FOWER PESSOAS
TRANS. COLIN BRAMWELL. REVIEWED BY DAVE COATES

Bramwell specifies that *Fower Pessoas* contains versions or re-writings, like Don Paterson's takes on Rilke in *Orpheus*, rather than "faithful" translations. Bramwell's Black Isle Scots lexicon is a good fit for Pessoa's existentialism, even if the unrelenting bleakness occasionally slips into parody. Pessoa's dreamy lyricism is here too and what's beautiful in the originals remains so in Bramwell's reworkings. There's a notable appetite for creative language-play in Scotland today, and *Fower Pessoas* is a worthy addition to the conversation.

CARCANET PRESS | £14.99 | PBS PRICE £11.25

TOM SASTRY: LIFE EXPECTANCY BEGINS TO FALL
REVIEWED BY SHASH TREVETT

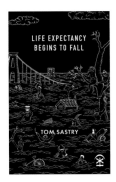

Tom Sastry's third collection anticipates the apocalypse: whether environmental, financial, military or societal. It examines our need to form uneasy, uncomfortable, compromised allegiances. In a collection which speaks so cleverly of the beautifully complicated, ignorant and heedless world we live in today, Sastry returns insistently to the promise of hope: a counterbalance affirming that only this will give us a "chance of life beyond the crisis", allowing us to participate in a new world, one day at a time.

NINE ARCHES PRESS | £11.99 | PSB PRICE £9.00

RACHEL SPENCE: DAUGHTER OF THE SUN
REVIEWED BY DAVE COATES

The first section of Spence's maternal elegy is a sonnet sequence of snapshots and still lifes; the poet's mother shines through here, hard-headed, stubborn and self-reliant to a fault. In the second, a long re-telling of the Medea myth, Spence allows her imagination to take the wheel. Here, despite the occasional drift into mythical abstraction, the depth of the poet's grief and admiration is clearly and movingly expressed. Spence's careful staging of an arduous, painful relationship is a poignant tribute.

THE EMMA PRESS | £9.99 | PBS PRICE £7.50

PÁDRAIG Ó TUAMA: KITCHEN HYMNS
REVIEWED BY DAVE COATES

Ó Tuama is a generous, painterly writer, and his attunement to the fragile, beautiful things of the natural world, and the sharp, painful things of the human, are at the heart of this collection. Its long middle section – a series of theological puzzlings rendered as short dialogues – I found less satisfying than his less abstract observations. *Kitchen Hymns* holds a tremendous amount of pain in its lines, but Ó Tuama seems to thrive in the careful handling of turbulent feelings.

CHEERIO POETRY | £12.00 | PBS PRICE £9.00

WENDY ALLEN: PORTRAIT IN MUSTARD
REVIEWED BY MEGAN ROBSON

Wendy Allen's latest pamphlet is an indulgence of openness, a celebratory clamour of sexuality, sensuality, and longing. References to fruit, flowers, make-up products, and fashion houses appeal to the senses and accompany a glinting humour, which is cut across with uncertain shame and an anxiety about loneliness. This confident work is confessional and intimate, but it is also a bold and explicit manifesto for women's desire, as bright and hot as mustard.

SEREN BOOKS £6.00

CATHERINE AYRES: JANUS
REVIEWED BY MEGAN ROBSON

Here, poems are postcards from the past. Catherine Ayres possesses a true gift for unique imagery and turn of phrase; memories crystallise in her hands. But Janus looks forwards as well as back, and "the present holds the past inside its heart." ('February 2014 – a trip to Edinburgh to see the Louise Bourgeois exhibition'). Deeply powerful and affecting, Ayres' poetry reminds us that where there is loss, something else may be gained, as in the masterful opening sonnet: "this square of sun that wasn't there before."

INDIGO DREAMS PUBLISHING £8.00

SLOW BURN: JORDI DOCE. TRANS. PAUL O'PREY
REVIEWED BY ALICE KATE MULLEN

Slow Burn precisely and surreally embodies each scene, "the body *is* this sunlit town-square". Doce's poetry moves, with such fluidity, through streets and forests to a house where "tedium rifles through the wardrobes", before ripping the rug from beneath our feet and revealing "there's a room missing". With the sudden surrealness of loss, his poems draw us into a space, which he carefully builds and demolishes before our eyes. In this ever-shifting world, Doce urges us to appreciate the slow, bright, burn of life, "this beautiful now and always".

BROKEN SLEEP BOOKS £8.99